Amber &

Dear
Beloved

SACRED MESSAGES
TO THE WORLD

Dear Beloved

SACRED MESSAGES
to the
WORLD

AMBER CHAND

DEDICATED
TO OUR WORLD

Prelude

T his sacred journey began with a stirring, a whisper, an internal nudge.

A year ago, sitting under the shade of a wisteria tree, my sketchbook in hand in my ninety five year old mother's English garden, I quietly began to draw simple mandala designs beckoned by their sacred geometry. The process was unselfconscious. I was not seeking perfection—my pen flowed, colors emerged, and I was lost in the quiet calm of a solitary summer afternoon.

I continued this practice in the following days and then something remarkable happened.

After each mandala was completed, I would close my eyes and slip into quiet meditation. It was out of this stillness, that certain messages—like silent wisps of ephemeral thought—began to arise, each a response to questions many of us have about the confusion and uncertainty of our times. Spilling onto the pages as if guided by an invisible hand, they were like pure drops of rain — clear, gentle and wise.

Like lanterns on a new path, these images and messages touched me deeply, reminding me that even in the midst of the profound challenges we all face in our world, it is the inner spirit of resilience, courage, vulnerability and vision that will help us navigate through these turbulent times.

I had to learn this lesson early in my life. As an Indian child, born into the sheltered world of privilege in the warm tropics of Uganda, I was lovingly nurtured by my mother and father and given the foundations of a generous and happy life. But by the time I was in my early twenties, this once secure world came to a terrifying end under the cruel and tyrannical dictatorship of Idi Amin Dada, who expelled all Indians out of his country, giving us only ninety days to leave before we would be shot on sight.

In an instant, my world crumbled and I lost everything. Our bank accounts were frozen, our

beautiful home on *Kololo Hill* was confiscated,
and my father soon died of a broken heart.
I had become an impoverished refugee, a global
nomad, a woman without a home. Standing
in the rubble of personal despair, I sought
desperately to answer one question: what will
become of me now?

This poignant question is for many at the
heart of our deepest yearnings and fears today.
What will become of us now? If, we have lost
our way, how will we find it? In the second part
of this book, I invite you to explore your own
journey as you read the affirmations, design and
color your own mandalas and reflect more deeply
on the lanterns that guide you on your journey.

In the end, dear reader, this book is a call to
love, to remembering who you are, to coming
home to yourself.

Be brave,

Amber Chand

PART ONE

Sacred Messages
to the World

THEY SAY:

We Have Lost Our Way

Journey into your life

Journey into your life
As a traveler,
A wayfarer.

Seek not to settle down too securely
For then you desire permanence
And become anchored
By the illusion of stability.

Like the river
Life must flow
It cannot be stopped.
Even as you bind it, trap it,
Try to imprison it with your
Stubborn resistance.

Even then
Life will find a way to seep
Through the cracks
And flow into the stream
Of your being.

She cannot be held back.
For change is her nature
Impermanence her cloak.

The traveler understands this.

THEY SAY:

How Shall We Know
What to do Next?

By not knowing

By not knowing.

For this is now a new time.
A time when
With trembling knees
And stirring hearts
We step across the abyss
And arrive at a new place.

A place unfamiliar to tired eyes
But home
To those who see.

THEY SAY:

We Are Afraid

Be not afraid

Be not afraid.
For what is fear
But a cloud of imaginings?

Beware of being enslaved
For fear is a cunning mistress
Seeking dominion
Over you.

Greet her like an old friend
Fluid and restless
But don't hold on so tight
Let her go.

Don't you see?
She is merely passing through.

THEY SAY:

We Feel Vulnerable

Just as the snowdrop

Just as the snowdrop
Opens up quietly after the
Storms of winter
So your tender heart
Now seeks to emerge.

Put down your armor
The one that barricades your heart.
Open yourself up
Even as you tremble
And gaze upon your weary world.

Let your vulnerable self
Become your shield.
For this journey is not for the
Faint hearted.

Be Brave.

THEY SAY:

We Are Confused

Don't you realize

Don't you realise
When you think too much
You become tight
Like a ball of smoldering fire
Ready to explode?

Loosen the grip of your mind
It is exhausted.
Listen now to the
Whispers of your soul
That seek to penetrate
The walls of your mistrust and doubt.

Step into the Dance of Life
As she spirals around you
Inviting you to move into the deeper
Pulse of your shared
Humanity.

Remember,
You are not alone.

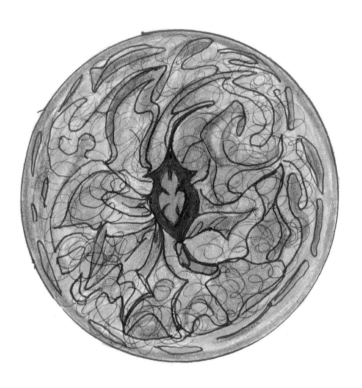

THEY SAY:

We Are Restless

Your restlessness

Your restlessness
Is that of the pacing tiger
That lies hidden within the
Shadowy corridors
Of your mind.

Settle down, be still.
Your restless pacing
Does nothing but
Fill up the sacred spaciousness
Of each precious moment.

Why do you not understand
That this searching is futile?
There is nothing to find.

The secret is all here
Within you.

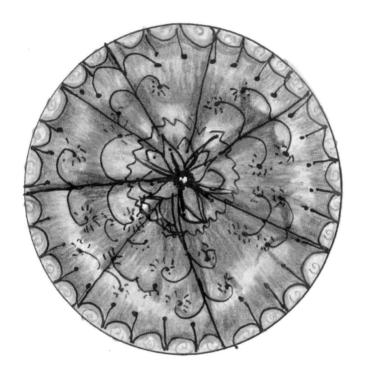

THEY SAY:

Don't You See Our Heart is Breaking?

Let your heart break

Let your heart break into a thousand pieces
For this is a time of dissolution and chaos.

Remember
Without the breaking heart
There is no path to healing.
Without embracing your collective pain
There is no recognition of Life.

For was it not Goddess Durga's sword
Piercing the heart of the Demon King
That allowed the flowers in your world
To blossom once again?

Let your heart break
A thousand times.

Let your healing begin.

THEY SAY:

Tell Us About Our Healing

You are already healed

You are already healed
Already whole.
Drop the veils and see with the
Eyes of remembrance.

You feel broken
By the stories that once
Wounded and diminished you.
They are only stories.
Tell a new one.

You are the source of your reality.
You are the creator of your world.
You have simply forgotten.

Find yourself now
Return to your home.
Be whole. Be healed.
Be held.

THEY SAY:

How Will We Find Love?

Love hides behind

Love hides behind
The veils of the heart
Love is shy.

She needs to be enticed
To sit at the table
To feast with you
To sip the wine of communion.

Love requires a sincere invitation
Come, come, you must say,
We await you.
For our hearts are smiling
At the promise
Of your arrival.

Love lights up.
She seeks only to shower
Her luminescent gaze
Upon your awakened heart.

She asks for nothing
But for you to welcome her.

THEY SAY:

Tell Us
About Our Future

Let go of the shackles

Let go of the shackles of your weary past.
Let go of the invisible chains
That bind you to the wounds of
Betrayal and abandonment.

Look instead at the horizons
Of your unfolding journey.
Scatter the golden seeds of
Possibility.
Dance into the beckoning arms
Of your Becoming.

Let the caterpillar dissolve into
An ocean of liminal possibility.
Let the butterfly soar into blue skies.

Come, discover this new world
Birthed in the presence
Of your fearless imagination.

Come.

THEY SAY:

How Will We Find Our Way Now?

Be still

Be still so that you can hear
Be open so that you can receive
Be clear so that you can see
Be kind so that you can serve
Be Love so that you can
Hear Life's call.

These are the lanterns that will
Light your way
Into this new
Time.

Trust the journey
It is now your Guide.

THEY ASK THE MESSENGER:

Tell Us Who You Are?

I am hidden, find me

I am hidden, find me
I am subtle, experience me
I am invisible, sense me
I am veiled as Maya, discern me.

I am the passing cloud, behold me
I am the vast blue sky, be awed by me
I am the woman adorned with sapphires, admire me
I am the beggar that seeks alms, be kind to me.

I am the myriad fish in the sea
The roaming animals in the forest
The soaring birds in the sky
Appreciate me.

I am the Beloved.
And you will always find me
Residing in your heart.
Don't you see?

I AM YOU. YOU ARE ME.

Remember

You are a Light in Our World

PART TWO

Sacred Messages
to Myself

Dear Reader,

May the affirmations on these next pages
guide you well on your journey. See them
as gentle lanterns on your path, each an
illumination that supports the spirit of your
deepest inquiry. Affirmations are intentions, a
silent vow to oneself to live into a way of being
that reflects kindness, generosity, gratitude
and compassion for ourselves and our world.
Be gentle with yourself.

Each affirmation comes with a *mandala*
(a Sanskrit word for circle that symbolizes
unity and harmony) that is left blank so that
you can pick up your coloring pens and play,
open to the surprise of what will emerge. I
invite you to not seek perfection or to judge
yourself as you explore this wordless realm of
creativity. See it as a silent doorway into your
soul's yearnings. Open the door, let your pen
flow, enjoy the experience.

Be brave.

I am open to the Journey

I see with new eyes

I let my fears
pass through

I walk
the path of healing

Dear Beloved

I open like a snowdrop

I listen to
the whispers of my soul

I discover
the secret within me

I am held
by Life's embrace

I welcome
Love's luminescent gaze

I scatter the
golden seeds of possibility

I hear Life's call

I am a light in the world